AN ACTIVITY
BOOK FOR KIDS

# ALL ABOUT CARS

FIRE
EXTINGUISHER

STOP

EXIT →

GO TRAVEL

· JACK SCUDDER ·

FARM
665
ROAD

All About Cars
An Activity Book for Kids
Text Copyright © 2024 by Jack Scudder
Cover design by Nicky Scott
www.nickyscottdesign.com
Book design by Frances Mackay
www.francesmackay.com

First Edition, July 2024


ISBN 979-8-9886723-6-4

Scout & Company Publishing
www.victoria-scudder.com

# CONTENTS

4    About This Book
5    Types of Cars
6    World's Earliest Automobiles
8    Car Design
10   Parts of a Car
12   Workshop Rules
14   Safety Equipment
16   Auto Repair Tools
18   How an Engine Works
20   How to Check the Oil
22   Types of Tires
24   Engine Coolant
26   How to Wash a Car
28   How to Pack a Car
30   Road Traffic Signs
32   License Plates
34   Brake Fluid
36   World Famous Car Races
38   Automotive Technician Interview
40   How Gasoline Is Made
42   Car Brands
44   Auto Aerodynamics
46   The Dashboard
48   Windshield Wipers
50   Tire Pressure
52   Micro Cars
54   Exhaust System
56   Vehicle GPS
58   Car Safety
60   Car Maintenance Log
62   About the Author
64   Answers and Image Credits

# ABOUT THIS BOOK

This activity book is designed to supplement the **Jack's Garage** series of books though it can easily be enjoyed and completed as a stand-alone.

The pages include practical information about a variety of car-related topics along with corresponding (and printable!) activities.

The workbook is designed for kids ages 8-12 to reinforce Jack's lessons about basic vehicle mechanisms.

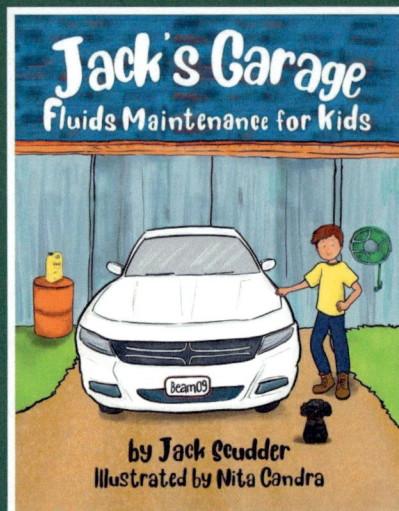

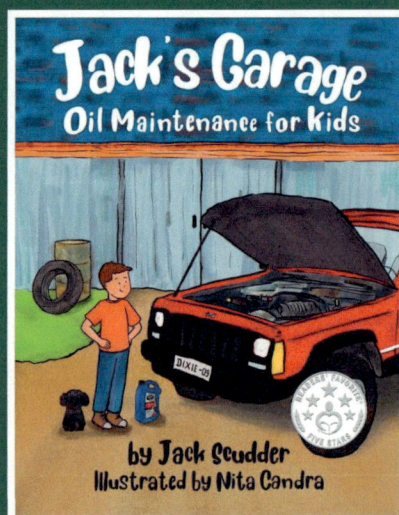

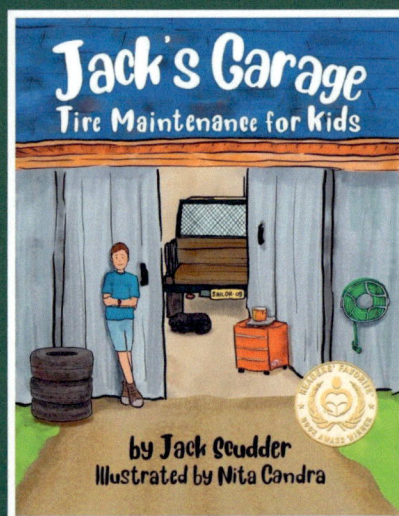

## A message from Jack

I was lucky enough to have a father who encouraged me to learn about car maintenance from the age of 4, and I want to help other kids learn too.

Jack's Garage
Fluids Maintenance for Kids
by Jack Scudder
Illustrated by Nita Candra

Jack's Garage
Oil Maintenance for Kids
by Jack Scudder
Illustrated by Nita Candra

Jack's Garage
Tire Maintenance for Kids
by Jack Scudder
Illustrated by Nita Candra

# TYPES OF CARS

sedan

pickup truck

SUV

micro car

convertible

sports car

off-road

super car

luxury car

electric car

mini van

muscle car

RV/ caravan

# WORLD'S EARLIEST AUTOMOBILES

In 1769, Nicolas-Joseph Cugnot invented the first steam-powered automobile.

In 1886, Carl Benz produced a gas-powered three-wheeled vehicle.

The first company formed to exclusively build automobiles was Panhard et Levassor in France, in 1889.

In 1890, Gottlieb Daimler and Wilhelm Maybach formed a company which later merged with Benz to form Daimler-Benz, and the Mercedes-Benz brand was born.

The Peugeot company was formed in 1891.

In 1893, the first American automobile manufacturing company was formed - the Duryea Motor Wagon Company.

In 1897, Ransom E Olds pioneered the car assembly line for his Oldsmobile cars. In the same year, Autocar Company was set up which remains the oldest motor vehicle brand in the USA.

In 1908, Henry Ford set up the Ford Motor Company which revolutionized automobile production with its affordable mass-produced Model T Ford.

Cugnot's steam-powered vehicle

Carl Benz's three-wheeled vehicle

1904 Oldsmobile

1918 Model T Ford

# History of Earliest Cars

Use the information on page 14 to complete this time line.

**1769** Nicolas-Joseph Cugnot invented the first steam-powered automobile.

**1886**

**1889**

**1890**

**1891**

**1893**

**1897**

**1908**

# CAR DESIGN

## Automotive Design

Automotive design is the process of developing the appearance and function of new vehicles.

The design team begin by creating a series of drawings. The drawings are sent out for people to review and make comments.

Digital models are made of the design and once these have been improved, quarter-scale and finally full-scale clay models are created.

**Full-scale clay model of concept car, Opel Monza, Germany**

**1938 Buick, an early concept car**

## Concept cars

A concept car is a car made to showcase new styling or new technology.

They are often exhibited at motor shows to gauge customer reactions.

**2008 BMW Gina concept car**

**1960 Cadillac Cyclone concept car**

**Concept car, Bertone Birusa, 2003. Never intended to go into production - just a styling exercise.**

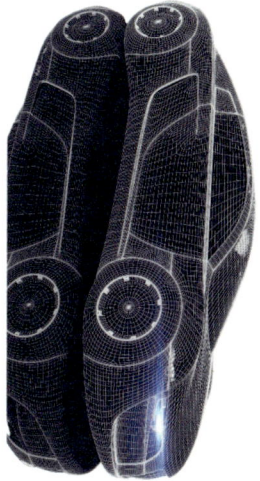

# Design A Car

Design your own concept car!
Draw it here.

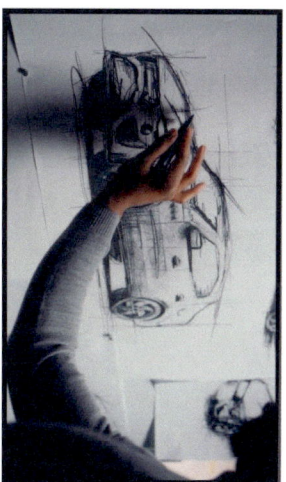

# PARTS OF A CAR

The names of the parts of a car can be different in different countries. Here are some of them.
Do you know of any others?

| | | |
|---|---|---|
| trunk | | boot |
| hood | | bonnet |
| windshield |  | windscreen |
| license plate |  | number plate |
| gas cap |  | petrol cap |
| backup light |  | reverse light |
| gas pedal |  | accelerator |
| tail pipe |  | exhaust pipe |

# Car Parts

Label the missing parts of this car.

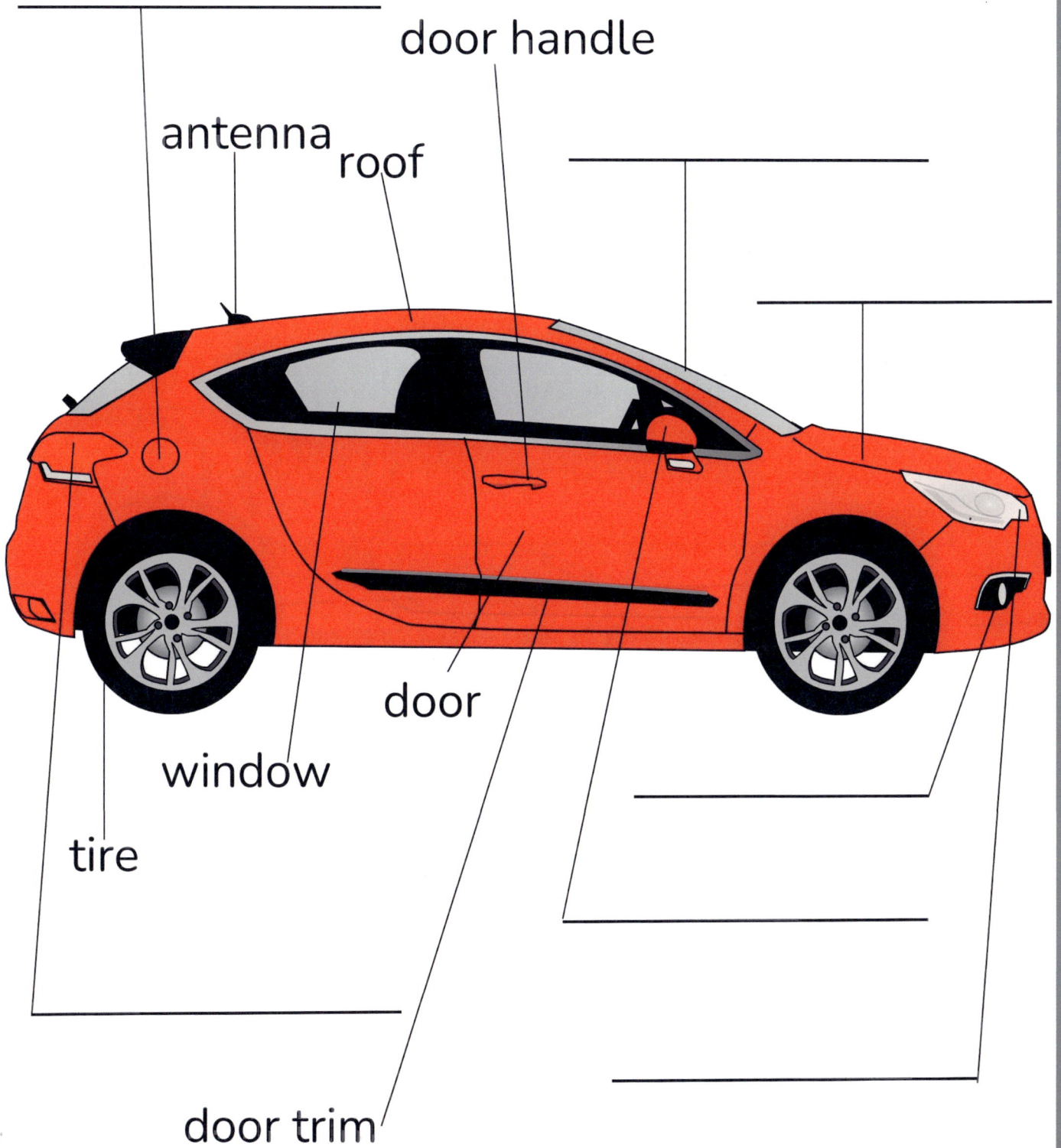

_____

door handle

antenna
roof

_____

_____

door

window

tire

_____

_____

door trim

# WORKSHOP RULES

## Remember these rules to keep yourself and others safe in the workshop.

Keep work areas clean and organized. Pick up tools and use tool cabinets to keep walkways clear and free from clutter.

Never wear loose clothing or clothing that is ripped or torn, it can get caught in machinery or tools.

Wear protective gear – eye goggles, gloves, and ear protection should be worn when making certain types of repairs.

FIRE EXTINGUISHER

Always disconnect the battery when working on electrical systems and near/around electrical wiring.

Make sure there is an up-to-date fire extinguisher in the workshop.

HOT!

Never place hands, tools, or other objects near the engine while it is running.

Always remove the keys from the ignition switch. Never leave the key in the ignition switch, as the key can draw an electrical charge from the battery.

Never work underneath a vehicle unless it has been properly supported.

# Design A Workshop Rules Poster

Use the information on page 10 to help you design a workshop rules poster.

# SAFETY EQUIPMENT

## Safety equipment to use when working in or visiting an auto workshop.

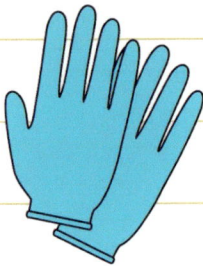

### Rubber Gloves
Rubber gloves not only keep your hands clean but also protect them from chemicals that can cause harm to your skin.

### Protective Eye Goggles
Goggles shield your eyes from debris, metal shavings, and splashing liquids.

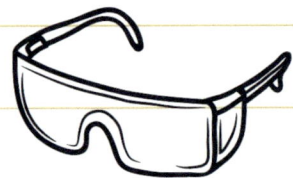

### Fire Extinguisher or Fire Blanket
Up-to-date fire extinguishers are a must for any home workshop.

### Ear Protectors & Dust Masks
Use ear protectors whenever you use or are standing near loud machinery or tools. Dust masks are essential when there are toxic fumes or lots of dust.

### First Aid Kit
Make sure the First Aid Kit is kept fully stocked - and know where it is.

# Workshop Safety

Sort the list into 'safe' and 'not safe'.
Write them in the correct column.

first aid kit is easy to find

tools are stored away

fire extinguisher is up to date

water on floor

tools lying on floor

ladder not secured

boxes stacked near door

items stored on shelves

trash is regularly cleared

floor is swept

hose is not wound up

nails on floor

| safe  | not safe ✗ |
|---|---|
| | |

# AUTO REPAIR TOOLS

| item | use | image |
|---|---|---|
| allen keys or allen wrenches | Used to drive bolts and screws with hexagonal sockets in their heads. | |
| hammer | Used to break things or knock things in. | |
| pliers | Used to hold, squeeze, and bend things. | |
| screwdrivers | Used to tighten screws and have different heads depending on the type of screw. The two most common are Phillips head and flat head. | |
| multimeter | Used to check electrical currents and voltages using metal prongs and a display. | |
| retractable knife | Used for cutting wires and tubes or opening new packages with supplies. Also called a box cutter. | |
| flashlight | Used for inspecting dark and deep parts of the car that normal lights can't access. | |
| wrenches | Used to tighten or loosen bolts that are in a place where a socket can't fit. | |
| car jack | Used to lift a car to access the underside using a hydraulic piston or a scissor design. | |
| impact wrench | Used for loosening and tightening lug nuts on wheels and stuck bolts using an electric motor or air pressure. | |
| electric drill | Used for tightening screws faster and tighter or using drill bits to make holes. | |

# Automotive Repair Tools

Complete the crossword puzzle using the clues.

**Down**

1 the name given to a knife that retracts back into the handle
3 an instrument used to measure electric current
4 a tool for lifting heavy objects such as a car
6 a tool used to provide grip to turn nuts & bolts
8 a tool used for holding or bending objects or cutting wire

**Across**

2 a tool with a heavy metal end used to break things or drive in nails
5 a small hand-held light powered by battery
7 a tool used to make holes
9 a tool with a flattened end or cross-shaped tip that fits into a screw to turn it

# HOW AN ENGINE WORKS

A four-stroke engine works by first turning the key that supplies power to the coil and starter.

Then, when the starter spins, it starts shooting air and fuel into the combustion chamber using a carburetor or fuel injectors.

All the valves then close, and the spark plug that is managed by the coil and distributor sparks. This causes the highly explosive gas to slam the piston down and produce rotation movement to the crankshaft.

This process is repeated extremely fast and causes a four-stroke engine to run.

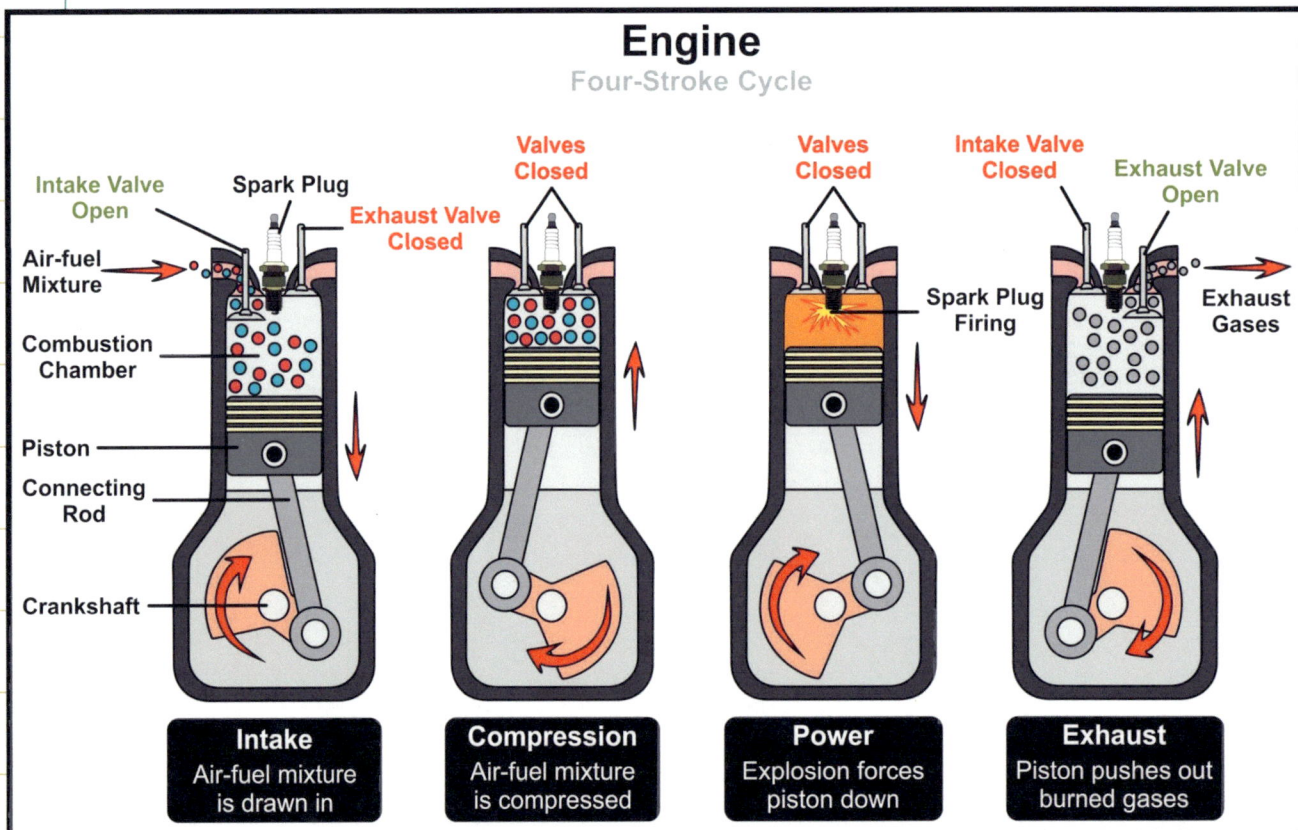

## Engine
### Four-Stroke Cycle

| Intake | Compression | Power | Exhaust |
|---|---|---|---|
| Air-fuel mixture is drawn in | Air-fuel mixture is compressed | Explosion forces piston down | Piston pushes out burned gases |

Intake Valve Open — Spark Plug — Exhaust Valve Closed — Air-fuel Mixture — Combustion Chamber — Piston — Connecting Rod — Crankshaft

Valves Closed

Valves Closed — Spark Plug Firing

Intake Valve Closed — Exhaust Valve Open — Exhaust Gases

# Engine Puzzle

Find these words in the puzzle.

compression  fuel  engine  closed
open  valve  piston  explosion  gases
four stroke  exhaust  crankshaft
combustion  air  starter motor

```
U G A S E S V M Q D K T E Q E F E B
C O M B U S T I O N A Q W W Z O I Q
E X P L O S I O N C L O S E D U O Q
L D Q F N G O K S P I J R K G R Z V
C O M P R E S S I O N G V Y Z S K M
X P P W K L I M V E N G I N E T D M
V S A I S T A R T E R M O T O R B Z
A I G I S C R A N K S H A F T O Y F
L E R O R T Y Q D M Q I N Z V K K U
V W R F U Q O K X U O P E N D E D E
E O Y A R C Y N X N S K D I E F K L
N U U B Q O C E X H A U S T Q J P D
```

# HOW TO CHECK THE OIL

Making sure your engine has clean oil (and enough of it) will help your engine function smoothly.

Dirty oil in an engine will cause its internal parts to wear out.

It's also important to have the right level of oil. Too little oil will decrease the lubrication and cause friction. This can cause serious engine damage.

**Why it's important**

**How to do it**

**1**

You will need motor oil. Your engine's oil type often is printed on the engine oil cap under the hood. If not, check your engine's manual. The most common type is 5w-30.

Next, open and brace your vehicle's hood. Once the hood is secure, locate the dipstick and pull it up and out. It should have some oil on it.

**2**

Use a rag to clean off the oil, then replace it.

**3**

Next, pull it out again slowly and look at the markers on the dipstick. The oil level should be between the lines.

**4**

FULL AND CLEAN OIL

LOW AND DIRTY OIL

# Design A Motor Oil Brand

Look at these oil containers.

Some are modern and some are vintage.

Invent a new brand of oil.  Design and color the container.

# TYPES OF TIRES

There are different types of tires for different kinds of road surfaces, vehicle types and weather conditions.

**Passenger tires** are designed for standard passenger vehicles. They are the most common type of tire and are used on normal road surfaces for a smooth and quiet ride.

**Off-road tires** have a deeper tread to provide more traction on unpaved surfaces such as loose dirt and mud.

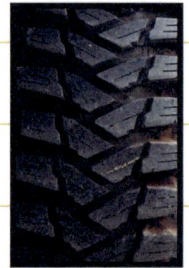

**Slicks** are what race cars use to gain maximum traction on roads. They are completely smooth tires with no grooves to give them more grip and are for dry-weather use.

**Snow tires** are street tires but with a little more traction and sometimes have little metal studs that can help driving on snow and ice.

**Chained tires** are for really deep snow and thick ice. They are often only used by truckers because they are impractical for today's cars.

**Trailer tires** are not designed for cars. They have minimal grip because the trailer is being pulled and not driven. Trailer tires have a narrower width and stiffer sidewalls.

# Match the Tires

Match the correct tire to each vehicle, terrain, or weather condition. Some tires may have more than one match.

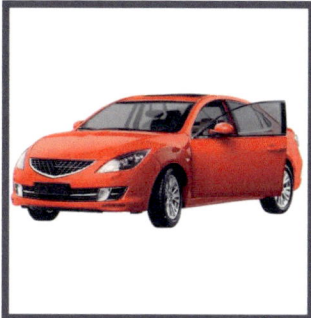

# ENGINE COOLANT

Coolant is a very important fluid for your car's radiator. The radiator cools the engine.

You need to make sure you have the correct coolant for your car.

**1**

Different vehicles require different coolant types. You can find the type for your vehicle in your owner's manual. Be sure you use the correct one to avoid damage to your radiator.

**2**

DO NOT OPEN THE CAP WHEN HOT !

Where do I put the coolant?

**3**

145 kPa
21 psi

When you open the engine hood, locate the coolant reservoir and look for the cap. It usually has a yellow symbol with "kPa" or "psi."

**4**

To check the coolant level, look on the side of the tank. It should say "max" and "min," which stands for maximum and minimum. Make sure the coolant level is on "max" mark.

MAX
MIN

# Engine Cooling System

Label the missing parts of the engine cooling system using words in the box.

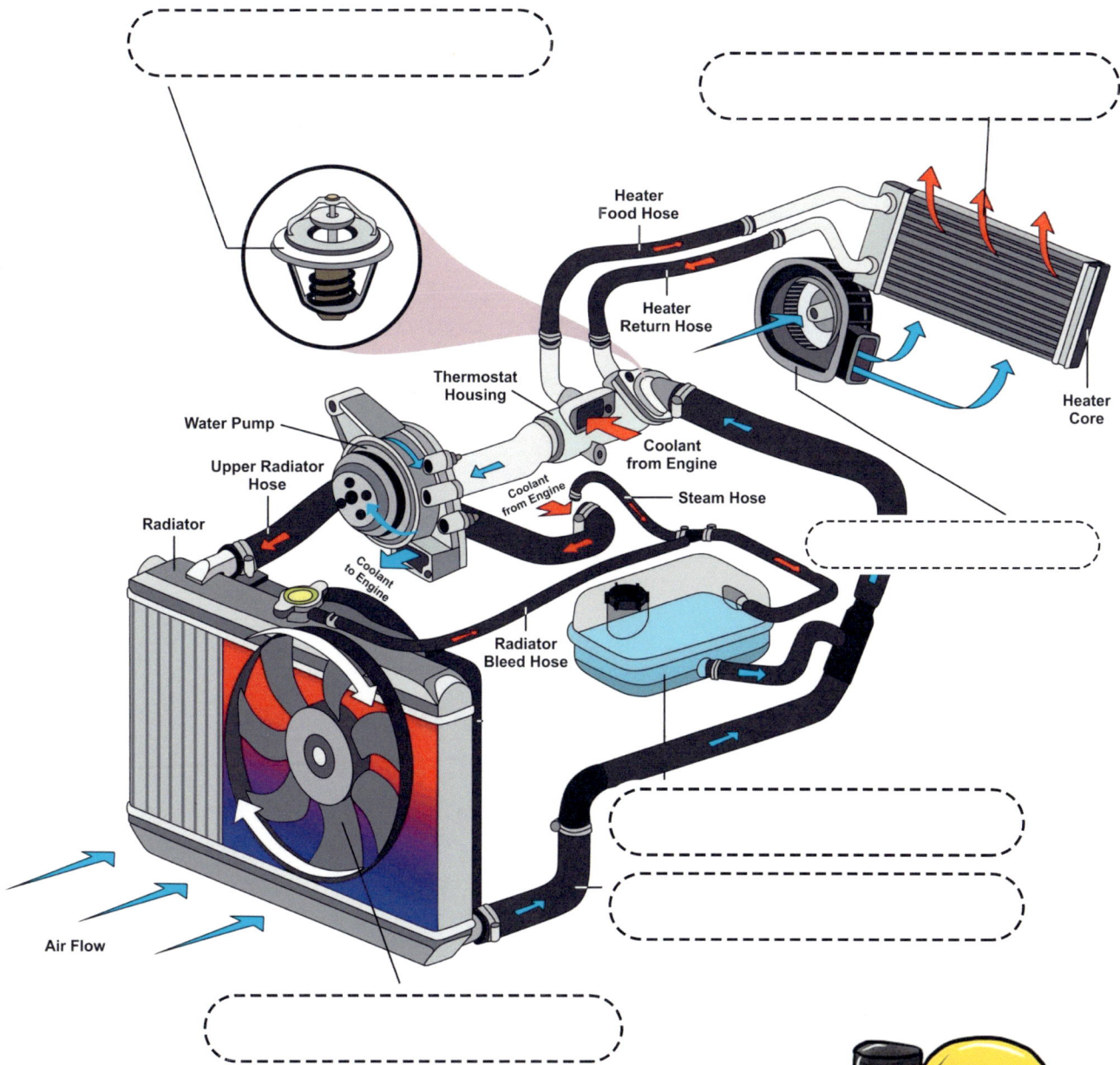

Heater Food Hose

Heater Return Hose

Thermostat Housing

Water Pump

Upper Radiator Hose

Radiator

Coolant from Engine

Coolant to Engine

Coolant from Engine

Steam Hose

Heater Core

Radiator Bleed Hose

Air Flow

| thermostat | radiator hose |
| coolant tank | radiator fan |
| hot air flow | fan |

# HOW TO WASH A CAR

**What you need**

When washing your car, you will need car washing soap and a clean sponge that is only used for your car. A good soap will protect the paint from fading. (Don't use dish soap!)

For cleaning your tires, use either a soft brush or a separate sponge from the one you use for the exterior.

You will also need a bucket with water, a water hose, and a microfiber cloth or clean towel.

## What to do

1. Spray the whole car down with water before you begin washing.

2. Put a little bit of car soap in the bucket. Then fill the bucket with water. You don't need a lot of soap!

3. Starting at the front of the car, use the sponge to rub away the dirt. Be sure to clean thoroughly while working your way all around the car

4. Rinse off the car with the hose. If you see any missed spots, use the sponge to clean them and then hose the car down again.

5. Next, use the tire brush (or extra sponge) to clean the tires and rims This part can get really dirty. Rinse each tire as you go so that you catch any areas that you missed.

6. When you have finished cleaning all parts of the car, rinse again.

7. Use a microfiber cloth or a clean towel to dry off the car.

# Jack's Car Wash Business

Use the information in Jack's Car Wash advertisement to answer the questions.

**JACK'S CAR WASH**

## PRICELIST

| | |
|---|---|
| Car | 10.00 |
| SUV (Average) | 15.00 |
| SUV (Large) | 25.00 |
| Pick Up Truck (Small) | 15.00 |
| Pick Up Truck (Large) | 25.00 |

How much will it cost the customer if Jack washes two cars? _____

How much will it cost the customer if Jack washes one car and one small pick up truck? _____

How much will Jack earn if he washes five cars in one week? _____

Jack washed four cars, one large pick up, and one average SUV last week. How much did he earn? _____

What vehicles might Jack have washed if he earned 40.00 last week?

_____

# HOW TO PACK A CAR

Remember these things to make sure you pack your car safely for a road trip.

Large or awkward shaped items, such as sporting equipment, are best stored on roof racks as long as they're not too heavy.

Make sure pets are securely strapped or in a pet carrier.

Large, heavy items should be packed at the bottom of the trunk and as far forward as possible to keep the center of gravity low and optimize weight distribution.

Put small items in suitcases/ boxes. Loose objects in your vehicle can become dangerous projectiles in a crash. Consider investing in a net or safety partition to prevent items from flying forward.

Ensure you have clear vision through your front and rear windshields and mirrors.

If you must store luggage in the cabin, use spaces beneath passenger seats.

Keep the area around the driver's feet clear

Pack an emergency car kit in case of breakdowns.

# Find the Items

This is how NOT to pack a car for a road trip!
Find the 10 items hidden in the picture.

GO TRAVEL

# ROAD TRAFFIC SIGNS

**STOP**

There are different colors used in road signs to indicate different purposes.

**ONE WAY →**

**SPEED LIMIT 5**

**Black & White**
These are used to show road laws such as speed limits.

**Yellow**
These are warning signs such as slow down, caution.

**DETOUR →**

**ROAD CLOSED AHEAD**

**Orange**
These are used for road works.

**REST AREA ↗**

**P PARKING ↔**

**H HOSPITAL**

**Blue**
These are used to show services such as hospital, food, gas.

**Green**
These help vehicles reach their destination - such as exit signs.

**EXIT 191**
**64 WEST**
**Lexington Charleston ↗**

**E MAIN ST**

**STOP**

**Red**
Warning signs - stop, do not enter, wrong way.

**Brown**
These are for leisure, historical or cultural locations.

**HISTORIC CALIFORNIA US 80 ROUTE**

**↑ ROCKY MTN NATL PARK**

# Road Traffic Signs

Circle the correct sign in each row.

| | | | | | |
|---|---|---|---|---|---|
| no right turn | | | | | |
| pedestrian crossing | | | | | |
| danger of falling rocks | DETOUR | SLOW | | | |
| road narrows | STOP | | | | |
| no u-turn | | | | | |
| hazard | | | | | |
| uneven road | | | | | |

# LICENSE PLATES

*Scenic* IDAHO
4C F6879
• FAMOUS POTATOES

A vehicle registration plate is called a **license plate** in the US, a **licence plate** in Canada, or a **number plate** in the UK, Australia, and India.

France was the first country to introduce registration plates in August, 1893.

In the US, each state issues their own plates. New York State issued the first US plates in 1903.

**United Kingdom**       **Tasmania, Australia**       **Mexico**

**Canada**               **India**                    **Bolivia**

# License Plates

Design your own license plates!
It could be for the state where you live or somewhere else.
Decide if you will have pictures as well as numbers.

# BRAKE FLUID

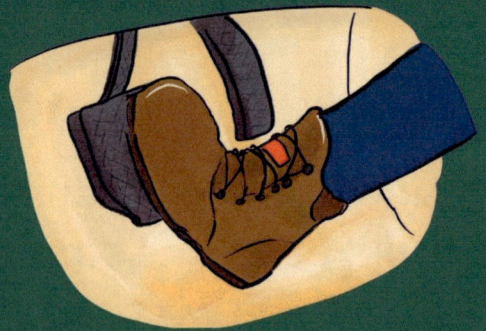

**Why it's important**

The purpose of brake fluid is to pressurize pistons to push the brake pads against the rotors that are located on the wheels.

What do the rotors do? They are metal disks inside the wheel (located on the axle) that spin with the car.

Wheel hub

Brake pad

Caliper

Rotor (disc)

When you press the brake pedal, it forces fluid from the brake master cylinder to the calipers.

Pistons inside the calipers push brake pads against the rotor, which slows down your vehicle.

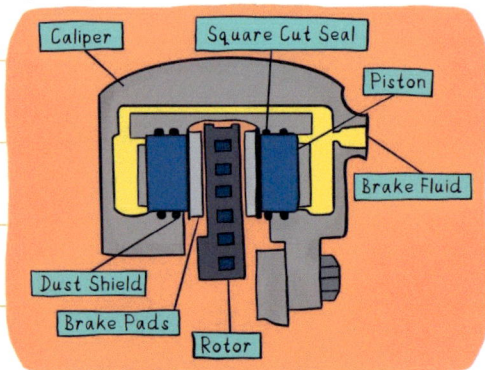

Caliper

Square Cut Seal

Piston

Brake Fluid

Dust Shield

Brake Pads

Rotor

**PADS NOT APPLIED**

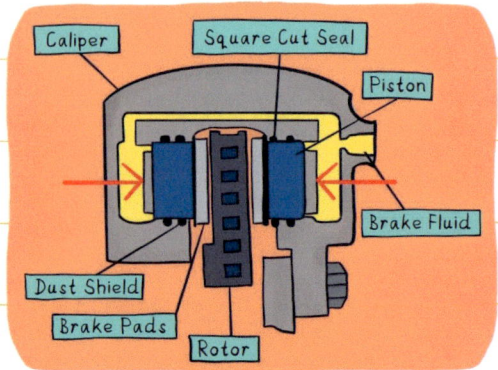

Caliper

Square Cut Seal

Piston

Brake Fluid

Dust Shield

Brake Pads

Rotor

**PADS APPLIED**

# Car Stopping Distances

This chart shows how far a car travels once the brakes have been applied at certain speeds.

| mph | km/h | | | |
|-----|------|---|---|---|
| 20 | 32 | | → | 17 ft / 5 m |
| 30 | 48 | | → | 37 ft / 11 m |
| 40 | 64 | | → | 67 ft / 20 m |
| 50 | 80 | | → | 104 ft / 32 m |
| 60 | 96 | | → | 150 ft / 46 m |
| 70 | 112 | | → | 204 ft / 62 m |
| 80 | 129 | | → | 267 ft / 82 m |

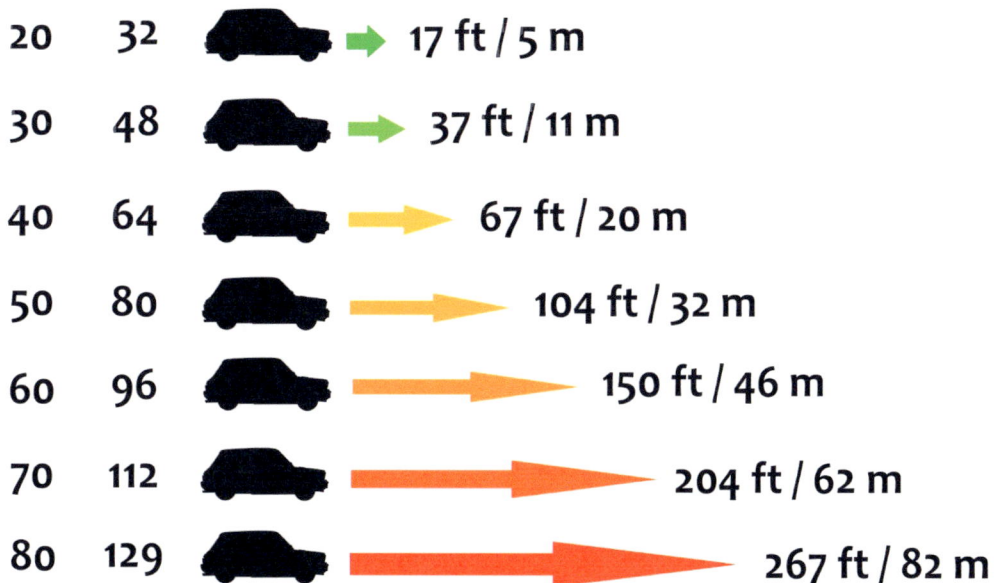

Check all the things you think will affect how long it takes for a car to stop once the brakes have been applied.

| | | | |
|---|---|---|---|
| driver's thinking time | ☐ | tiredness of driver | ☐ |
| how worn the tires are | ☐ | speed of the car | ☐ |
| road surface condition | ☐ | age of the driver | ☐ |
| mass of the car | ☐ | if headlights are on | ☐ |
| number of windows in the car | ☐ | if driver has taken alcohol | ☐ |
| weather conditions | ☐ | if driver is distracted | ☐ |

# WORLD FAMOUS CAR RACES

### Dakar Rally

Dakar is an annual off-road endurance event. It began in 1979 and originally ran through southern Europe and Africa, ending in Dakar in Senegal. From 2009 to 2019 it was held in South America and from 2020 it has been held in Saudi Arabia. The race includes motorbikes, quads, cars, UTVs and trucks.

Dakar Rally, Peru, 2018

Formula One cars
from 1949 - 2001

### Monaco Grand Prix

The Monaco Grand Prix is a Formula One race held annually on the Circuit de Monaco. The event has been running since 1929 and is considered by many to be one of the most important and prestigious automobile races in the world.

### Indianapolis 500

The Indianapolis 500, or Indy 500, is an annual event held at Indianapolis Motor Speedway in Indiana. The race has been running since 1911. Cars that enter are single-seat, open cockpit purpose-built race cars.

Indy 500 race start - 2007

# Design a T-Shirt

Design a T-shirt for car racing fans. Color it in.

# AUTOMOTIVE TECHNICIAN INTERVIEW

**Q** Why did you decide to become a automotive technician? Not many girls choose this job.

**A** My father showed me how cars work from a very young age. I used to pull things apart and put them back together again when I was little - so I love fixing things.

**Q** What is your favorite type of vehicle to work on?

**A** I like working on older cars because they are very simple and have well-known and easy technology.

**Q** How do you approach challenges?

**A** If there is a challenge I approach it with logic and talk to other mechanics. Sometimes I look it up online.

# Workshop Coloring

Color the picture.

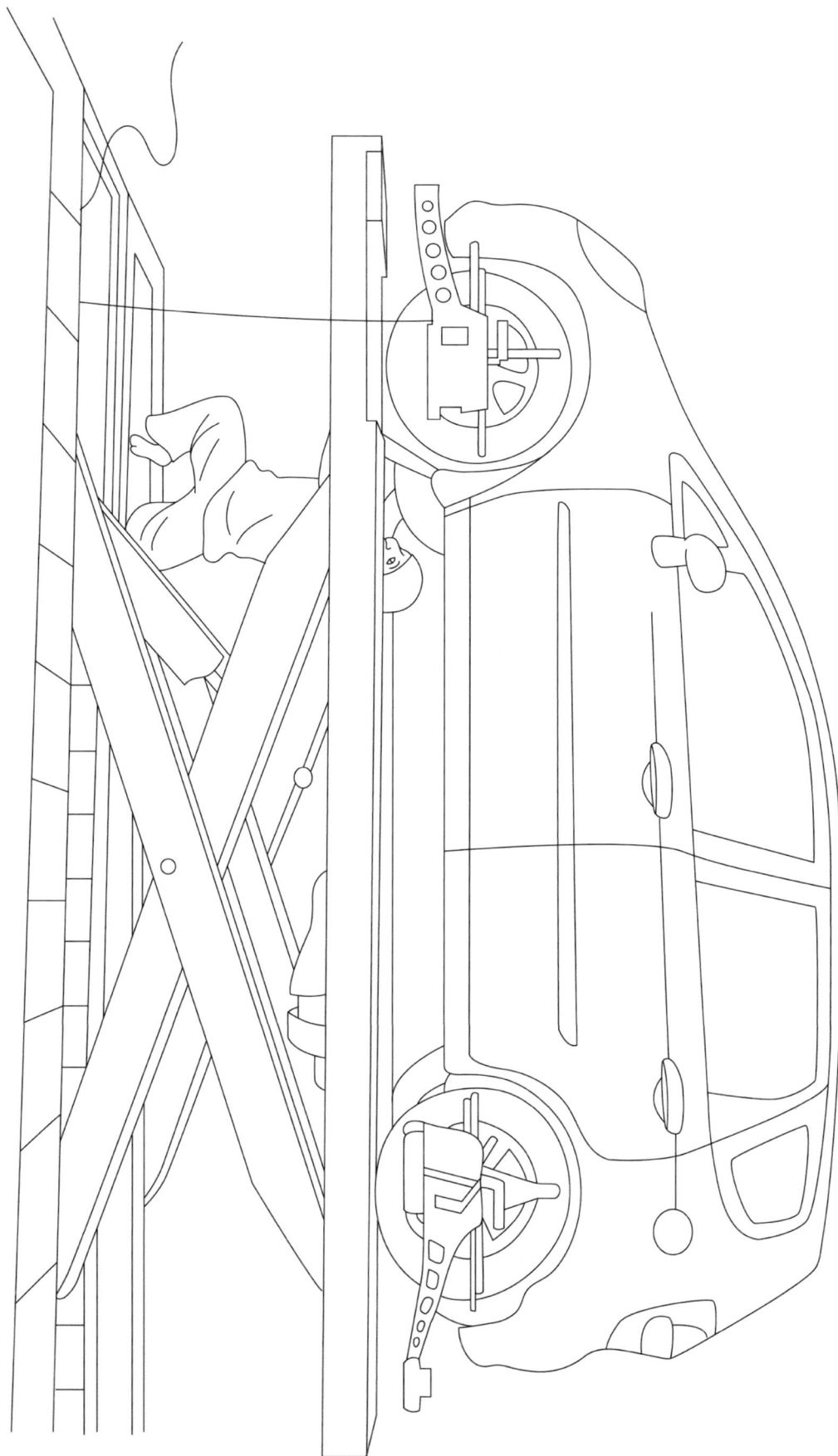

# HOW GASOLINE IS MADE

**Petroleum** is another name for oil, a liquid found deep underground. Oil is used to make gasoline, or petrol.

After the oil is pumped from the ground, it goes to large factories called **refineries**. There, the oil is heated to a very high temperature which separates it into various components, one of which is **gasoline**.

The gasoline is stored in large tanks and is treated before being sold to gasoline companies.

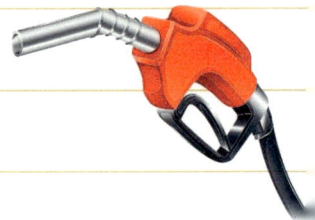

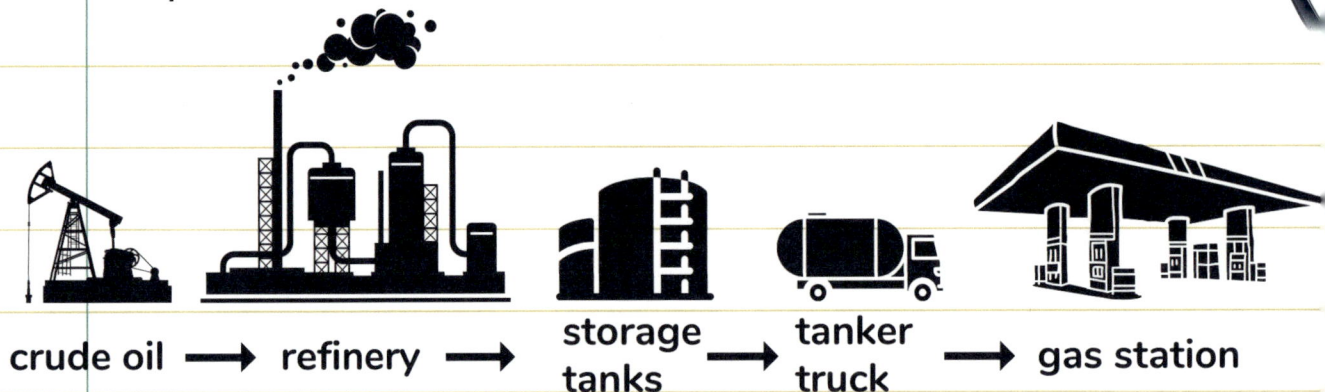

crude oil → refinery → storage tanks → tanker truck → gas station

GAS STATION

# Gas Station Maze

Get the car to the gas station, collecting both cans on the way.

# CAR BRANDS

Here are some well-known car brands from around the world. How many do you know?

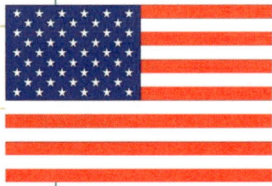

### United States
General Motors (Buick, Chevrolet, Cadillac) Ford, Jeep, Lincoln, Dodge, Hummer, Tesla, Rivian, RAM

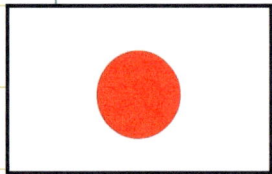

### Japan
Honda, Toyota, Mazda, Nissan, Subaru, Suzuki

### United Kingdom
Aston Martin, Bentley, Jaguar, Land Rover, McLaren, Rolls Royce

### Italy
Alfa Romeo, Ferrari, Fiat, Lamborghini, Maserat Lancia

### Germany
Audi, BMW, Mercedes-Benz, Porsche, Volkswagen

### Korea
Hyundai, Kia

# Car Brands

Find out the names of car brands around the world.
Write a brand for each letter.

| | | | | |
|---|---|---|---|---|
| A | | N | |
| B | | O | |
| C | | P | |
| D | | Q | |
| E | | R | |
| F | | S | |
| G | | T | |
| H | | U | |
| I | | V | |
| J | | W | |
| K | | X | |
| L | | Y | |
| M | | Z | |

# AUTO AERODYNAMICS

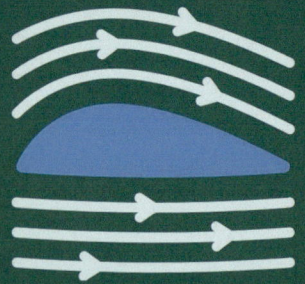

**Aerodynamics** is the way objects move through air.

**Drag** is a force that tries to slow things down. The shape of an object affects drag. The more air that hits a surface, the more drag it makes.

Edmund Rumpler's 1920 tear-drop shaped car, designed to reduce drag. Built in Austria.

Cars are designed to be as aerodynamic as possible to reduce drag and wind noise, and to prevent lift forces that cause instability at high speed.

Chrysler Airflow, 1934, the first American car to use streamlining.

As early as 1920, car manufacturers were trying to work out how the shape of a car affects drag.

Truck with added bodywork on top of cab to reduce drag.

A **streamlined** shape is one that has less drag. On a vehicle, this would be a low triangular hood (like a race car) rather than a boxy, rectangular front (like a dump truck)

A wind tunnel is used to calculate how aerodynamic a car is.

# Aerodynamics

Number these vehicles in order from most aerodynamic (1) to least aerodynamic (12).

☐

☐

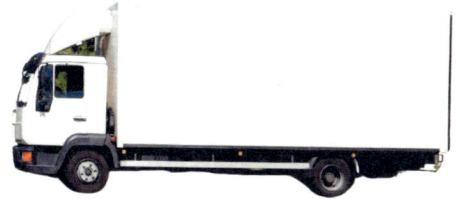

☐

☐

☐

☐

☐

☐

☐

☐

☐

☐

# THE DASHBOARD

A **dashboard**, or dash, is a control panel located directly ahead of the driver. It displays instruments and controls for the vehicle's operation.

The dashboard contains the speedometer, tachometer, odometer, engine temperature gauge, fuel gauge, turn indicators, seat-belt warning light, parking-brake light and engine malfunction lights.

The **speedometer** measures the speed of the vehicle.

The **tachometer** displays the revolutions per minute (RPM) of the engine.

The **odometer** measures the distance travelled by the vehicle.

# Dashboard Icons

Match these dashboard icons to their meaning.

airbag error

brake warning

low oil

trunk open

low fuel

anti-lock braking system

high beam indicator

hood open

low washer fluid

turn left signal

turn right signal

low coolant

parking brake

horn

battery

fog light

rear window defrost

windshield defrost

engine temperature warning

# WINDSHIELD WIPERS

**Windshield** (or windscreen) **wipers** are devices used to remove rain, snow, ice, water or debris from a vehicle's front (and sometimes rear) window. This ensures clear visibility for the driver.

A wiper usually has a metal arm with a long rubber blade attached to it.

The arm is powered by a motor. The speed of the wipers is usually adjustable.

Often, a **windshield washer** system is also used. This sprays water or a window washer fluid onto the window to help remove dust and dirt.

American inventor, Mary Anderson, patented a window cleaning device for electric trolleys and cars in 1903.

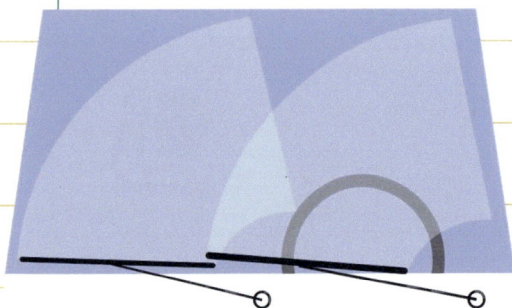

Most vehicles have this format of wipers.

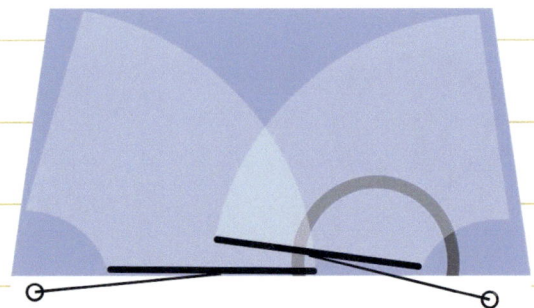

Some vehicles have this format of wipers.

# Windshield Wipers

Find these words in the puzzle.

arm  motor  washer  blade  rain
water  cleaning  rubber  window
clear  safety  windshield wipers
debris  snow  dirt  spray  glass  visibility

```
D  D  N  A  C  L  E  A  N  I  N  G  S  N  O  W  O  L
W  E  V  R  R  Y  Z  V  W  R  U  B  B  E  R  B  L  S
X  I  B  T  X  M  W  P  C  D  H  A  B  A  P  L  X  B
Y  W  N  R  Y  V  I  S  I  B  I  L  I  T  Y  A  R  Y
Y  O  F  D  I  L  P  W  M  R  U  R  W  Z  R  D  Y  C
I  L  Q  H  O  S  D  W  A  T  E  R  T  U  N  E  N  V
J  P  A  I  B  W  P  E  F  G  L  A  S  S  N  B  R  S
K  Q  W  V  D  R  A  I  N  I  X  K  C  L  E  A  R  P
W  I  N  D  S  H  I  E  L  D  W  I  P  E  R  S  H  R
S  A  F  E  T  Y  D  M  L  R  P  S  Y  T  V  B  J  A
R  S  M  O  T  O  R  L  C  V  W  C  C  U  Y  E  I  Y
D  I  Q  E  U  W  A  S  H  E  R  E  D  N  N  Z  Z
```

# TIRE PRESSURE

Ignoring tire pressure can cause uneven wear and imbalance, which can cause a blow out. The lower the pressure, the more dangerous it becomes.

With low air in the tires, your vehicle won't ride as smooth. Low tires can cause friction and this uses more gas. Your vehicle's speed will be slower too.

**How to do it**

You might be old enough to put air in the tires yourself, but always make sure an adult is with you. Remember, safety first!

You will need an air compressor. If you don't have one at home, you can usually find one at a gas station.

You'll also need a **tire gauge**. The **compressor** needs a special fitting called an air chuck.

1. Take off the valve stem cap. Don't lose it!
2. Attach the air chuck to the valve stem. Make sure it's tight.
3. Turn on the compressor to fill the tire. Stop often to check the pressure with the tire gauge.
4. When finished, put the cap back on.

How do you know if the tire pressure is right or wrong ? Look inside the door jam for the yellow sticker. It's on the driver's side. If you can't read it or if the tires aren't the originals, look on the sidewall of the tire itself.

**1**

**2**

**3**

# Match The Treads

Match the tire tread pattern to the correct tire track.

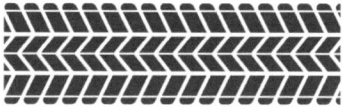

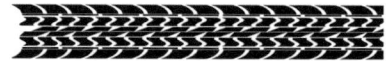

# MICRO CARS

**Micro cars** are the smallest of cars with 3 or 4 wheels and often an engine smaller than 700cc.

The first micro cars were manufactured in the UK and Germany after World War II and were called minicars. However, as far back as 1895, tricycles and cyclecars were made in Europe.

Micro cars are often covered by separate regulations than normal cars and they sometimes require a motorcycle license rather than a car license.

Peel P50, 1964 & Peel Trident, 1965, Isle Of Man

Messerschmitt KR200 bubble car, Germany, 1955-1964

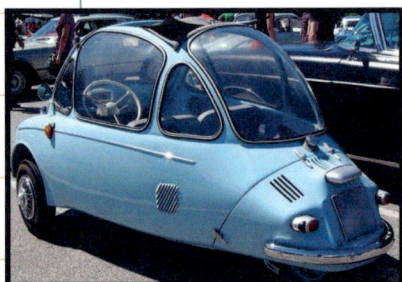

Heinkel Trojan bubble car, 1961

Fiat 500, 1970, Italy

Renault Twizy, 2012

Tango by Commuter Cars, USA, 1998, which is narrower than some motorcycles

# Micro Connect the Dots

Connect the dots from 1 to 34 to draw a micro car.
Color the picture.

Connect the dots
from 1 to 35 to
draw a micro car.
Color the picture.

# EXHAUST SYSTEM

The **exhaust system** in a vehicle is designed to carry away exhaust gases from the engine.

The piping that joins all the components of the exhaust system is called the **exhaust pipe**. An exhaust **flange** consists of a pair of metal sections that joins the exhaust pipe together.

exhaust system

A **manifold** is used to collect exhaust gas from two or more engine cylinders into one pipe.

manifold

A **catalytic converter** is used to reduce the amount of harmful emissions being released into the atmosphere.

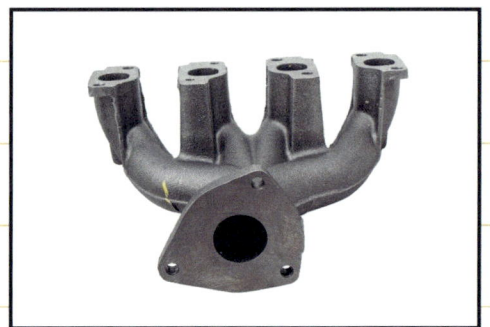

A **muffler** (or silencer) is designed to reduce the noise level.

muffler

A **Resonator** removes high pitched noises, hums, and buzzes.

# Exhaust System

Use the information on page 54 to explain what each part does. Write your answers in the boxes.

**flange**

**catalytic converter**

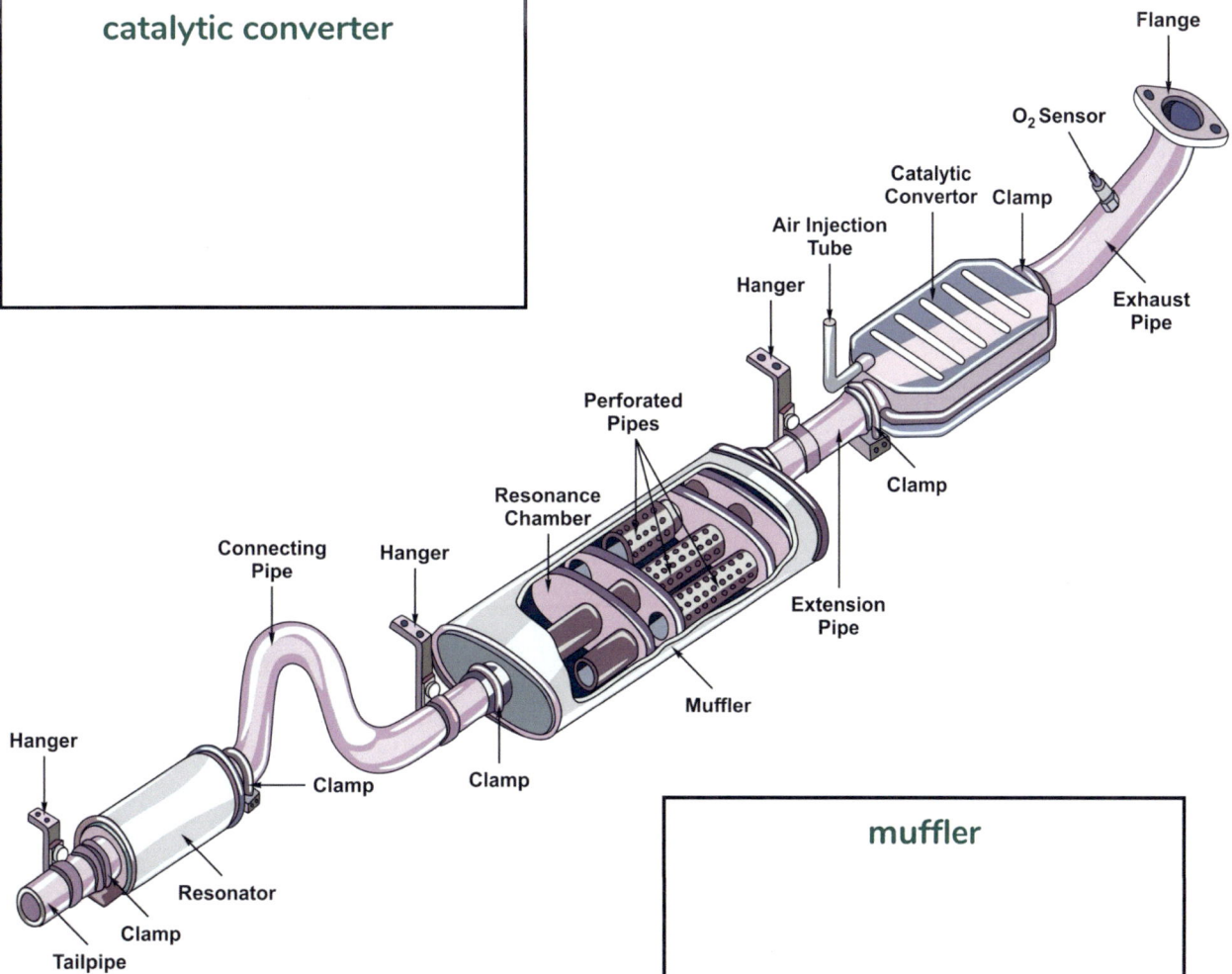

Flange

O₂ Sensor

Catalytic Convertor  Clamp

Air Injection Tube

Hanger

Exhaust Pipe

Perforated Pipes

Resonance Chamber

Connecting Pipe

Hanger

Clamp

Extension Pipe

Muffler

Hanger

Clamp

Clamp

Resonator

Clamp

Tailpipe

**muffler**

**resonator**

# VEHICLE GPS

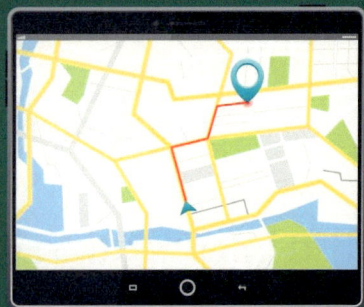

**GPS**, which stands for **Global Positioning System**, is a system that helps people navigate in the air, on land, and on water.

It consists of three components:

1. **Satellites** – send radio signals to Earth
2. **Ground stations** – monitor and control the satellites
3. **Receivers** – receive signals from the satellites

car GPS receiver

The GPS receiver in the vehicle receives radio waves from the satellite and displays the vehicle's location on a digital map.

satellites

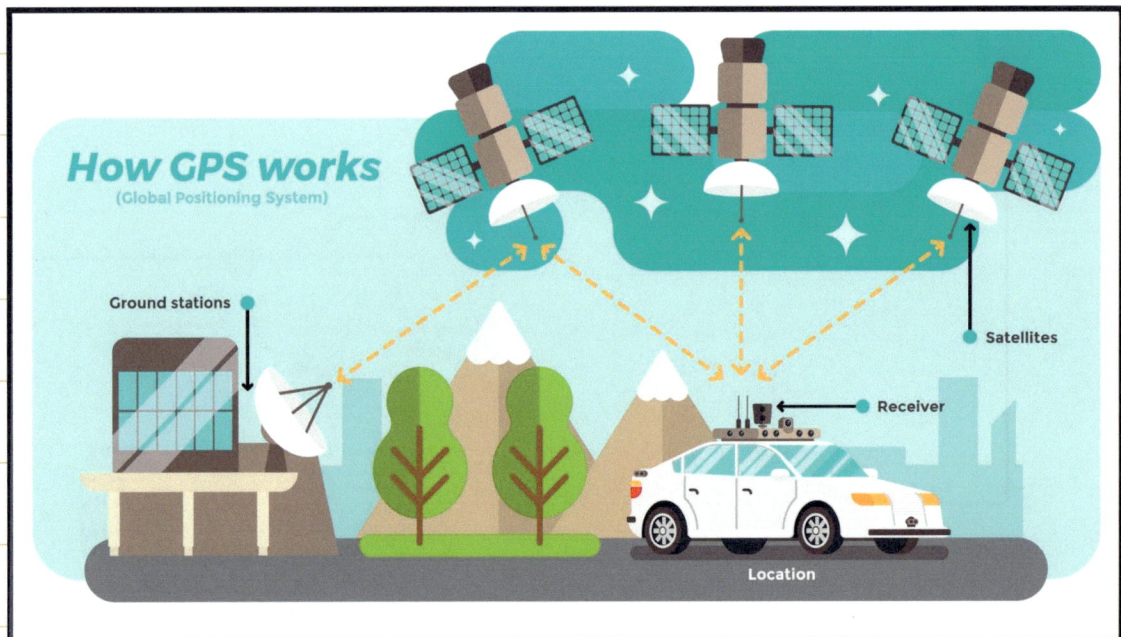

**How GPS works**
(Global Positioning System)

Ground stations

Satellites

Receiver

Location

# Map Directions

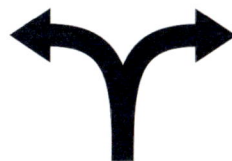

How well can you navigate?

Complete the directions to Ali's house using the map.

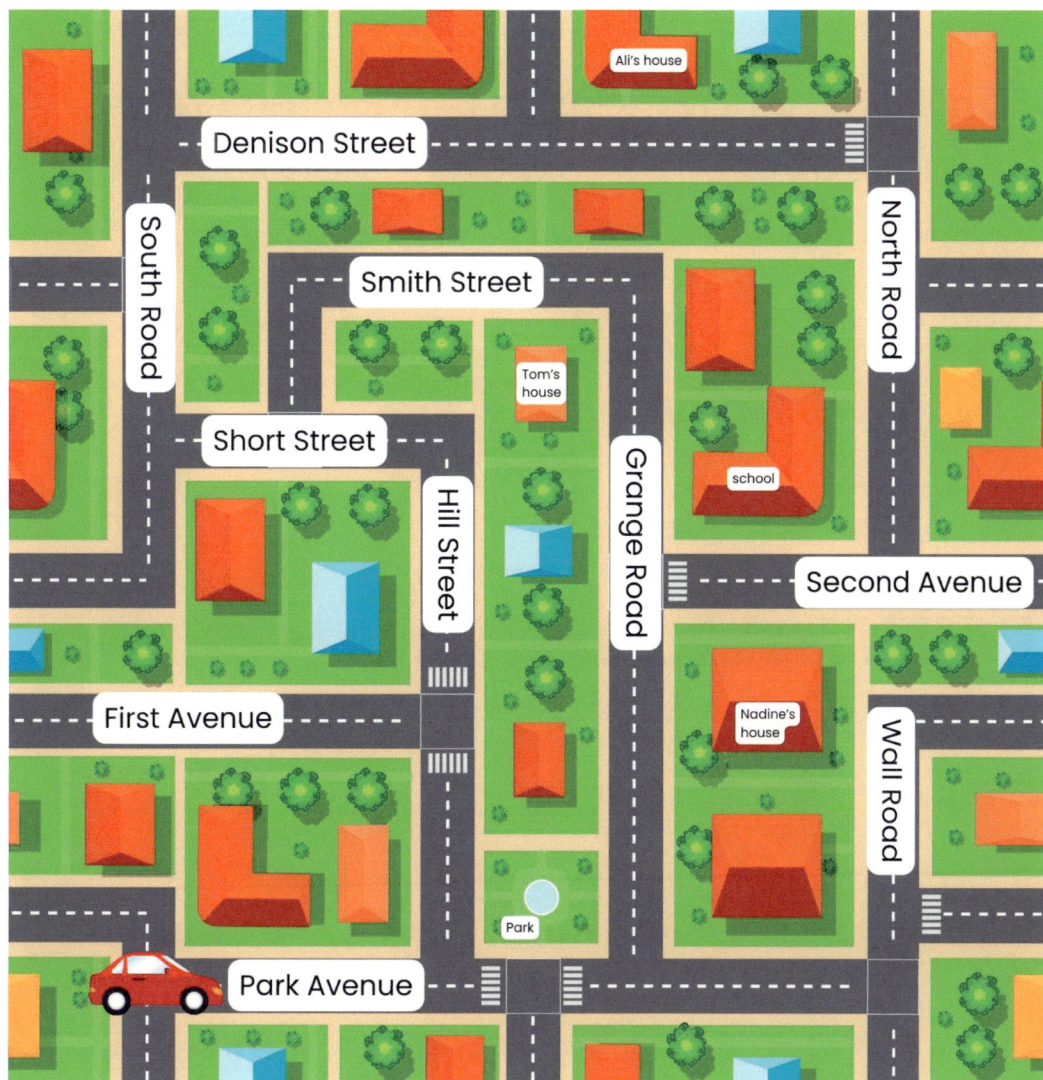

From Park Avenue, turn _____ into Grange Road.
Stop to pick up Nadine. Continue along Grange Road, past
the _____ on the right. Stop to pick up _____ .
Drive on and turn _____ into Smith Street. Turn left and
continue to _____ Street. Turn right and right again
into _____ Road. Turn right into_____
Street and continue until you get to Ali's house, which is on
the _____ .

# CAR SAFETY

Here's a list of handy items to keep in the car in case of a break down, unexpected conditions, or an accident.

**Spare Tire & Jack**

**Emergency Items**
roadside warning triangle, flares, car fire extinguisher

**First Aid Kit**

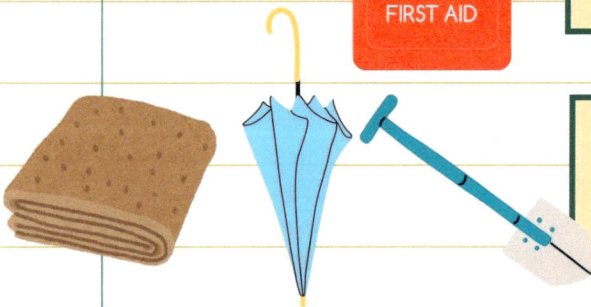

**Weather Items**
blanket, umbrella, folding shovel

**Vehicle User Manual**

**Food & Water**
Keep some drinking water & non-perishable food in the car.

**Tool Kit**
Include a flashlight, window breaker, seat belt cutter & multi-purpose tool

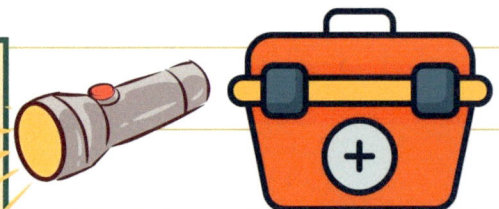

# Driving Safety

Look at these pictures and answer the questions.

This person is texting while driving. What might happen?

What should she do instead?

This person is feeling very sleepy while driving. What might happen?

What should he do?

This person's car has broken down. She doesn't have a phone. How might your family help her if you see her at the side of the road?

This person's dog is sitting in between the front seats. What might happen if the driver stopped suddenly?

How can pets travel safely in cars?

# CAR MAINTENANCE CHECKLIST

## Basic car safety checklist
- Seatbelts — check tension and belt buckle operation
- External lights — replace bulbs if necessary
- Handbrake — ensure that it can hold the vehicle on a slope
- Windscreens & mirrors — check for cracks
- Windscreen wipers — check wear on wiper blades
- Horn — ensure this works
- Fluids — check engine oil and engine coolant levels
- Tires — ensure tires are at the correct pressures; check treadwear
- Spare tire & jack — ensure they are operational; check toolkit

## Fluids checklist
- Engine oil
- Radiator coolant
- Brake fluid
- Power steering fluid
- Windshield washer fluid
- Transmission fluid
- Differential fluid

## Other general things to check
- Radiator hoses — check for leaks and cracking
- Engine air filter — check that it is clean
- Battery — look for corrosion around terminals
- Fan belts — ensure none are loose or squeaking on start-up
- Unusual engine noises — hard to start, ticking, hissing or clunking
- Ensure that child seats are fitted correctly

# Car Maintenance Log

**YEAR/ MAKE/ MODEL OF VEHICLE** _____

## CHECK EVERY MONTH

| ITEM | MONTH |
|---|---|
| Engine oil level | J F M A M J J A S O N D |
| Function of all interior & exterior lights | J F M A M J J A S O N D |
| Tires (including spare) for wear & pressure | J F M A M J J A S O N D |
| Windshield washer fluid level | J F M A M J J A S O N D |

| **EVERY 5000 MILES OR 10 MONTHS** | |
|---|---|
| Change engine oil & filter | |
| Rotate the tires & balance if needed | |
| Inspect brake pads, rotors, hoses & parking brake | |
| Inspect automatic transmission fluid level if dipstick present | |
| Inspect engine cooling system strength & hoses | |
| Inspect exhaust system & heat shields | |
| Inspect rear axle & U-joints, if equipped. Lubricate 'zerk' fitting. | |
| Inspect half-shaft boots | |
| Inspect steering linkage, ball joints, suspension, tire-rod ends | |
| **EVERY 20,000 MILES** | |
| Replace cabin air filter | |
| **EVERY 30,000 MILES** | |
| Replace engine air filter | |
| Change automatic transmission fluid | |
| Inspect brake fluid - change if discolored or aged (5 years max). | |
| **EVERY 100,000 MILES** | |
| Change engine coolant | |
| Change spark plugs & inspect coils | |
| **EVERY 150,000 MILES** | |
| Replace timing belt/ chain | |
| Replace drive/ accessory belts | |

## ✎ NOTES

Always follow the manufacturer's recommended maintenance schedule.

# ABOUT THE AUTHOR

Jack is the award-winning and best-selling author of **Jack's Garage: Tire Maintenance for Kids**, **Jack's Garage: Oil Maintenance for Kids** and **Jack's Garage: Fluids Maintenance for Kids**. He has big goals for his series! He wants to see more kids understand the inner workings of cars and trucks so that they know how to take care of them as they get older and start buying their own vehicles.

Jack started working on vehicles alongside his dad when he was about 3 years old. Even if he was just holding a screwdriver off to the side, he was carefully observing and asking a ton of questions. When Dad didn't know the answer, the two would sit side-by-side and look it up together.

Jack lives in Florida with his mom, dad, and Sailor the dog. He's a military kid and proud of it! Jack is a homeschooled teen and has been a Sea Cadet since he was 10 years old.

When he's not tinkering in the garage, he's tearing apart and rebuilding computers, gaming, and generally driving his mother crazy!

# WANT MORE BOOKS?

**Jack's Garage: Tire Maintenance for Kids**
Family Choice Award™ Gold Medal (2022)

Royal Dragonfly Book Award First Place
(2022) - Youth Author Non-Fiction

Royal Dragonfly Book Award First Place
(2022) - Transportation

**Jack's Garage: Oil Maintenance for Kids**
Readers' Favorite 5-Stars (2023)

**Jack's Garage: Fluids Maintenance for Kids**

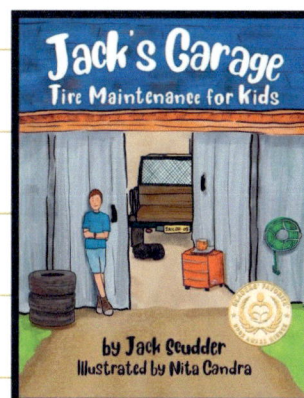

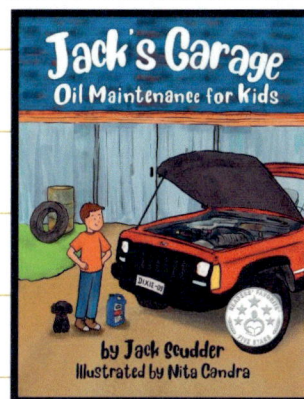

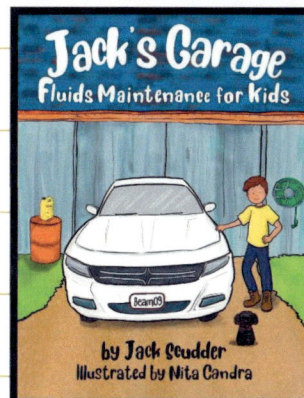

# REVIEWS

Your reviews mean a LOT to me as an
Indie author! Please take a moment to
log into Amazon and review my book.
This helps me get seen!
Make a kid happy - spread the word!

THANK YOU!

# Activity sheet answers

**P7** 1886 - Carl Benz produced a gas-powered three-wheeled automobile

1889 - Panhard et Levasson was the first company to exclusively build automobiles

1890 - Mercedes-Benz brand was formed

1891 - Peugeot was formed

1893 - the first American automobile manufacturing company, Duryea Motor Wagon Company, was formed

1897 - Ransom E Olds pioneered the car assembly line. Autocar Company was formed.

1908 - Henry Ford set up the Ford Motor Company

**P11**

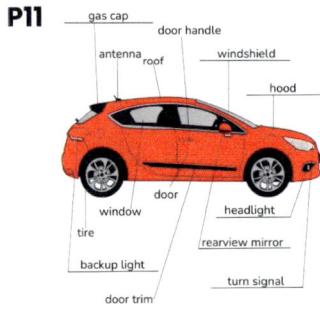

Labels: gas cap, door handle, antenna, roof, windshield, hood, door, window, headlight, tire, rearview mirror, backup light, turn signal, door trim

**P15** not safe = tools lying on floor, boxes stacked near door, hose not wound up, ladder not secured, water on floor, nails on floor

**P17**

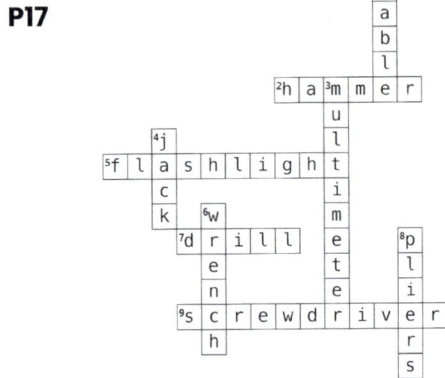

Crossword: retractable, hammer, jack, flashlight, multimeter, wench, drill, pliers, screwdriver

**P19**

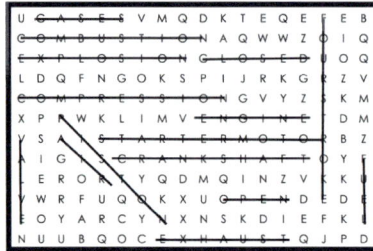

Word search: GASES, COMBUSTION, EXPLOSION, CLOSED, COMPRESSION, ENGINE, STARTERMOTOR, CRANKSHAFT, OPEN, EXHAUST

**P25**

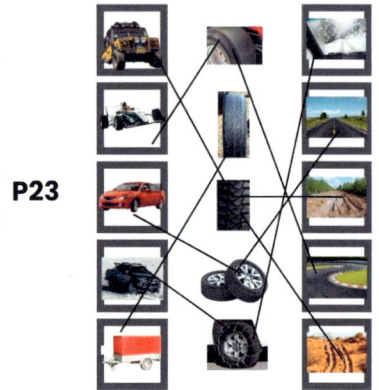

Labels: thermostat, hot air flow, fan, coolant tank, radiator hose, radiator fan

**P23**

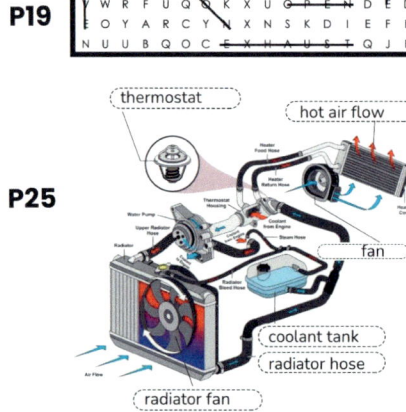

**P27** 20.00, 25.00, 50.00, 80.00   Possible answers include: 4 cars, 1 average SUV + 1 large SUV, 1 small pick up + 1 large pickup

**P29**

**P31**

no right turn
pedestrian crossing
danger of falling rocks
road narrows
no u turn
hazard
uneven road

**P35** All except number of windows & if headlights on

**P41**

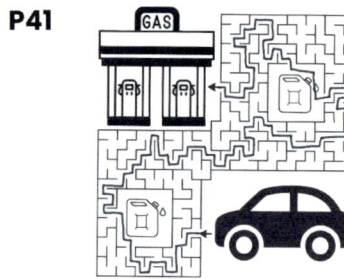

**P47**

airbag error
brake warning
low oil
trunk open
low fuel
anti-lock braking system (ABS)
high beam indicator
hood open
low washer fluid

turn left signal
turn right signal
low coolant
parking brake (P)
horn
battery
fog light
rear window defrost
windshield defrost
engine temperature

**P49**

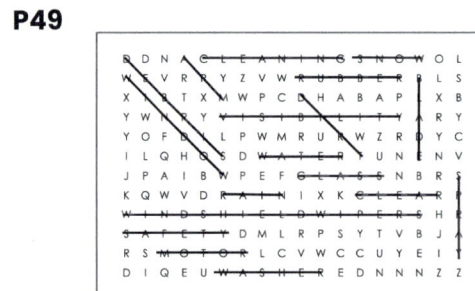

Word search

(64)

**P51**

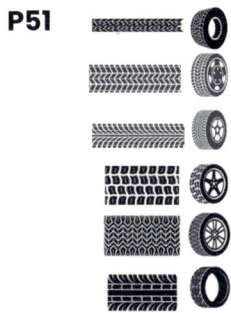

**P55** flange - a pair of metal sections that joins the exhaust pipe together
catalytic converter - reduces the amount of harmful emissions
muffler - reduces noise
resonator - removes high pitched noises, hums, buzzes

**P57** left, school, Tom, left, Short, South, Denison Street, left

**P59** Answers may vary:

texting - the driver is distracted and may have an accident
   driver should pull over where safe to do so, stop the car, text, then drive on
sleepy - a tired driver may fall asleep at the wheel and have an accident
   driver should pull over where safe to do so, stop the car and rest before driving on
broken down - ask if the driver needs help, offer to call friend/ family or breakdown service, wait until
      help arrives
unrestrained dog - the dog may catapult through the windshield if the car stops suddenly
      the dog could also distract the driver and cause an accident
      put the dog on the back seat and attach a harness

# Acknowledgments/ credits

**Page 5:**
mini van
https://commons.wikimedia.org/wiki/File:2019_Chrysler_Pacifica_Touring_L_3.6L_rear.jpg
Kevauto, CC BY-SA 4.0 <https://creativecommons.org/licenses/by-sa/4.0>, via Wikimedia Commons
**Page 6:**
Carl Benz three-wheeled vehicle
https://commons.wikimedia.org/wiki/File:Patent-Motorwagen_Nr.1_Benz_1.jpg
DaimlerChrysler AG, CC BY-SA 3.0 <http://creativecommons.org/licenses/by-sa/3.0/>, via Wikimedia Commons
Cugnot's steam-powered vehicle
https://commons.wikimedia.org/wiki/File:Joseph_Cugnot%27s_1770_Fardier_%C3%A0_Vapeur,_Mus%C3%A9e_des_arts_et_m%C3%A9tiers,_Paris_2015.jpg
Joe deSousa, CC0, via Wikimedia Commons
1918 Model T Ford
Photo 5961997 | Model T Ford © Margojh | Dreamstime.com
1904 Oldsmobile
https://commons.wikimedia.org/wiki/File:1904-oldsmobile-archives.jpg
The original uploader was DougW at English Wikipedia., Attribution, via Wikimedia Commons
**Page 8:**
Concept car design
https://commons.wikimedia.org/wiki/File:Bertone_Birusa_2003_1.jpg
No machine-readable author provided. ChiemseeMan assumed (based on copyright claims)., Public domain, via Wikimedia Commons
Opel Monza concept car – model
https://commons.wikimedia.org/wiki/File:Opel_50_Jahre_Design_(14541643013).jpg
Robert Basic from Germany, CC BY-SA 2.0 <https://creativecommons.org/licenses/by-sa/2.0>, via Wikimedia Commons
Buick concept car
https://commons.wikimedia.org/wiki/File:1939_..._Harley_Earl_and_%22The_Y_Job%22.jpg
{{{1}}}, CC BY-SA 2.0 <https://creativecommons.org/licenses/by-sa/2.0>, via Wikimedia Commons
Cadillac Cyclone
https://commons.wikimedia.org/wiki/File:1960_Cadillac_Cyclone_Concept_Car_Side.jpg
mashleymorgan from Alameda, CC BY-SA 2.0 <https://creativecommons.org/licenses/by-sa/2.0>, via Wikimedia Commons
BMW Gina
https://commons.wikimedia.org/wiki/File:BMW_Gina_Museum.jpg
ravas51, CC BY-SA 2.0 <https://creativecommons.org/licenses/by-sa/2.0>, via Wikimedia Commons
**Page 18:**
Engine diagram
Illustration 248111225 © Udaix4 | Dreamstime.com
**Page 21:**
Oil cans
Illustration 127460330 © Maksym Yemelyanov | Dreamstime.com
Oil cans vintage
ID31715358 © Lukeruk |Dreamstime.com
**Pages 22-23 & Page 51:**
Tires and tracks
Illustration 144428514 © Tartilastock | Dreamstime.com
Tire and track
Illustration 35156322 © John Takai | Dreamstime.com
Tire and track
Illustration 172007912 © Olga Kurbatova | Dreamstime.com
**Page 25:**
Coolant diagram
Illustration 248252297 © Udaix4 | Dreamstime.com
**Page 29:**
Find the objects in the packed car
Illustration 245105106 © Kharlamova | Dreamstime.com
**Page 30:**
Road signs
Illustration 29719731 © Breakers | Dreamstime.com
**Page 32:**
Tasmania number plate
https://commons.wikimedia.org/wiki/File:2008_Tasmania_registration_plate_A_22_ZJ.jpg
Zoundsalike, Public domain, via Wikimedia Commons
UK plate
https://commons.wikimedia.org/wiki/File:UK_Rear_Registration_Plate.png
ZElsb, CC BY-SA 4.0 <https://creativecommons.org/licenses/by-sa/4.0>, via Wikimedia Commons
Mexico plate
https://commons.wikimedia.org/wiki/File:Matr%C3%ADcula_automovil%C3%ADstica_M%C3%A9xico_2002_Sonora_VUK-17-75.jpg
Robinsoncrusoe, Public domain, via Wikimedia Commons
California
https://commons.wikimedia.org/wiki/File:California_license_plate,_August_2012.png
California DMV., Public domain, via Wikimedia Commons

Made in United States
Troutdale, OR
09/14/2024